THE GALLERY & MUSEUM SURVIVAL GUIDE FOR PARENTS

Turning Tantrum Throwers
into
Mini Art Lovers

By Jo Ebisujima

Published by Little Ebi Publishing

Copyright ©Jo Ebisujima 2014

All rights reserved.

ISBN-13: 978-0-9927079-2-7

Dedication

This book is for everyone out there who loves art, whatever the shape or form. To all the parents who are helping their children also fall in love with art and the importance it holds in our world.

And also to my family for supporting me, my son for inspiring me and to Di, Paige, Jacqui and Joanna who always have my back, no matter how crazy my next idea is! Last but not least Diane Aoto for her editing eye!

Why You Should Buy This Book

Art in whatever form is an important part of everyday life, everything that we use from milk cartons to arm chairs, have been designed with style and function in mind. So, it is important to introduce the love of art and design to the next generation so they can build on, improve and then invent the next generation of amazing design.

As you know, you were not handed a manual when you became a parent and sometimes you just need a bit of help or guidance to set you on the right track to get the most out of the next part of the journey - this quick read guide is intended to help you do that. Sensible, practical and do-able advice coupled with fun ideas, tricks and tips make it an invaluable addition to your library.

*Funny, I was just saying how much I'd love to go to museums again, then I find this little book! It's BRILLIANT and so simple!! I *ALSO* went to the free bonuses, and seriously, I'm floored and stoked. Literally I'll be looking for a museum for us to visit this week, armed with the bonus treasure hunt map + lovely ideas clearly shared by a mom who thinks of kids in a way that honors both the kids and the parents!*

Eva Rawposa

Contents

One Era Finished And Another Began...

For years I would while away a whole day just meandering around a museum or art gallery, soaking up the atmosphere and getting lost in my own thoughts, taking time to read every piece of information available and absorbing all the new snippets that I came across. Fast forward a few years, to the toddler-wrangling stage, and I started to think that my days of museums and galleries were going to be severely numbered.

I'm happy to say I was wrong; although trips out tend to be shorter, they are still fun-packed and I still manage to get my fill of arty goodness. All it took was to look at things from a child's point of view.

Museums and galleries are great for children, opening up their world to more magic and wonder. I have heard people say that they wouldn't dream of taking a child to a gallery until they are school age; all those years of enjoyment missed out on, what a shame. I think the younger you start the better; then they learn the rules as they grow and it becomes no big deal to take them along.

I am sure everyone has suffered at least one bad museum trip in their time. For me it was an old style, very formal museum, very much in the ilk of old things in glass cases with a small description, half of which was written in Latin. And a Victorian style educator of a father who made sure we paid attention by threatening us with "I'll be asking questions when we get home" which of course, he did! That phrase is now a standing joke in the family and thankfully I don't have to suffer those types of trips anymore.

Many museums and galleries have stepped into the modern world with audio guides and interactive displays but there are still those old-school museums out there; the sort that is all very dull unless you have an obsession with the artifacts on show. Your eyes glaze over and you start dreaming of a nice cold beer on the plaza...

Well, I imagine that is how many kids feel in a museum or gallery. Maybe not dreaming of beer, more likely ice-cream, but the sentiment is the same. There are things they are not allowed to touch and they don't really understand what they are or why they are important, they are not allowed to run around, jump or shout, can we get to the gift shop already?

Of course, as soon as the child gets bored, that is when they start to play up and your enjoyment of whatever you are trying to see goes straight out the window. Even the dullest of museums and galleries can be made fun though, read on to find out more...

What led me to write this book is that I know there are plenty of museum and gallery lovers out there who feel like they are missing out now that the kids have come along, but it really doesn't have to be that way.

I purposely kept this short, so you can dig in and get through it in one or two sittings, and then get out there and start enjoying your gallery-going life again. Not only that, you can pass on your passion to your kids because, after all, you are their greatest teacher.

The 10 Steps

To Fun Filled Trips

Before we get into the 10 steps, just a little reminder that all children are different, they all have different learning styles and what works well for one might not work for another. You know your child the best, use the book as a guide, pick out what will work with your child and leave the rest. Don't be afraid to experiment, try something new, a different approach can make all the difference! Try the different games and ideas, you will never find out what works and what doesn't for your kids if you don't! And of course, get them involved too, there are numerous game and activity ideas in the book but I bet your kids can come up with some great ones of their own.

Most of all, keep it fun. That is the only way anyone enjoys learning.

Last thing before we get started, the last couple of steps include lots of fun games and ideas on how to continue the conversation after your visit. You will also find a free resource pack that you can download here: http://bit.ly/GandMSG

I

Choose The Place Wisely

Is your intended destination a good fit?
Is it going to be really busy?

If you see that there is a special Monet exhibition on at your local gallery, before rushing off down there, check out the local reviews. There are online magazine sites in most cities that have a review section, check to see if the exhibition has set up a Facebook page or use Google to see what results you can find. Ask friends and family if they have been.
The first warning bells sound if the place is extremely busy; are people lining up for 2 hours to get in? When my son was about 6 months old we went to a da Vinci exhibit in Tokyo. It was an absolute nightmare. It was literally head-to-nose all the way round, shuffling speed and stifling hot. I had my son in a carrier but he was getting hot and grumpy and we ended up missing a whole chunk of the show. It was a lesson well learned and the situation could only have been worse if he had been a tantrum-throwing toddler.

Obviously weekends and public holidays tend to be busier, but if you are really desperate to see the show, call the gallery and ask them which time of day is usually the quietest. For most kids, going in early is the best plan; by lunch time they have had enough and are ready for their naps or quiet time Generally, most museums and galleries are at their busiest from noon to 3pm, so that time is best avoided if possible.

Also check the gallery website for free days or special family days and any special events that they are holding. Many places allow you to buy tickets in advance (although obviously this runs the risk of somebody getting sick on the day and having to cancel), or you could do it online before you leave the house. This might save you grumpy waiting-in-line time.

By checking in advance you can prepare yourself for the various scenarios that might pan out or make an educated decision on the best time of day or the best day of the week to visit.

When you are choosing where to go, ask yourself the questions...

- Is it going to be very busy?
- Is it likely to be fun?
- If it isn't child orientated, can I make it fun?
- How much time should we plan to spend there?

- Is that a reasonable amount of time for my child?
- Travel - will this affect the amount of time we can spend at the gallery?
- Do I need to take a packed lunch or can we eat there?
- If my child needs a break, is there somewhere they can run off steam nearby?

2

Do Your Research

How child-friendly a gallery is varies from place to place. Some don't allow kids under a certain age, while others are totally child-orientated. Getting on the galleries website is usually a good indicator: many of the large galleries and museums have a whole section of resources for children, some have special audio guides for kids and/or information sheets for them to use as they go round the museum.

Many places have human guides, either free or for a fee. You need to decide whether it would be worth your while hiring one and whether the guide is good with kids. Check the length of the tour: if it is 3 hours long then that is a good indicator that you should give it a miss if you have little ones.

Some places don't allow bags or strollers in the gallery itself so you may have to check them in; check the website for any rules before you leave and pack accordingly. Rules regarding food and drink are often very strict too.

If it is a large museum then plan ahead, find out what your child would like to see and aim to just find those pieces of work. Many of the world's top museums are enormous and trying to see everything is asking for disaster, so plan strategically to get the most out of your day. Obviously those world-famous pieces like the Mona Lisa always draw a crowd and are likely to be busy, so mixing it up, seeing a few important pieces as well as some lesser known artworks, will allow your family to move more freely.

Keep your plans realistic; a couple of hours are usually enough for little ones before they get fed up, half a day at the most. Don't try and fit in 'one more thing'; leave whilst everyone is still on a high and in good spirits. After all, you want this to be a positive experience.

The British Museum in London is a perfect example of how a museum should work. Although in set-up, most of the museum is pretty old-school (glass cases with old things in them!), they have embraced the idea that the youth of today will be their clientele of tomorrow. After digging around on their website I discovered they have information booklets for various sections of the museum. Ebi-kun (my son) really wanted to see the Egyptian section so as soon as we arrived, we went to the information desk and asked for a couple of the trail booklets.

I was happy about this because it meant I hadn't had to do any extra work and Ebi-kun loved the excitement of doing the trail. Inside they have to find various items and look for specific information, like a treasure hunt set in a museum. They are really well done and would be an excellent example for other museums and galleries to follow.

We did the Egyptians in great detail and then had a break. Afterwards we went on a treasure hunt to find a few famous pieces like the Sutton Hoo loot and the Lewis Chessmen. Handing the plan of the museum over to the kids and asking them to find the right room can add to the excitement (and amount of time you are in there if you are not careful!).

Find exhibits on topics that the child is interested in and you are onto a winner. Ebi-kun, like many kids, had been through a stage where he was obsessed with Egyptians and the pyramids. He got so excited when he saw the canopic jars which are used for storing the organs that I thought he might burst a blood vessel. Almost 3 years later and he still talks about it!

Which brings me to the next section...

3

Follow The Child

Follow the child is a phrase Dr. Montessori used, as she believed that in observing the child's interests we can develop their learning at a much deeper level. You are more likely to learn, enjoy and remember something if it is about a topic you are interested in, as I am sure you can attest to when you think back to your school days.

When a child already has an interest in something, say dinosaurs, their knowledge has usually come from books or TV programs, they already have some understanding of the subject matter and there is something in there that grabs their imagination. This is what you want to exploit in your museum and gallery trips.

If they already have a fundamental understanding, it is much easier for them to try and understand what is being presented. They can form questions and enquire more, know what to ask about and what to look out for. Often they will compare new information with things that they have already learned…

"Dad, my book on dinosaurs said that T-rex and Dimetrodon lived at different times, why are they together here?"

Often passionate collectors turn their collections into small museums that are not well-advertised. Try googling some specialty subject + museum + your location and see what comes up, you never know what hidden gems might be just down the road! These are usually a goldmine for little enthusiasts who have a specific obsession. I recommend doing the same when you are planning a trip too. I have often found that at these small places, the owners are more than happy to tell you all about their collection and you get far more out of it than if you were at a large, nationally-acclaimed museum.

I often get asked, how do you 'follow the child'? Well, most of the time you will already be switched onto it: your child gets excited at anything related to trains, or goes round the supermarket pointing out anything that has a ladybird on it. Maybe your child can spout off realms of facts about the stars or can talk your ear off about ponies. But sometimes it is subtler; maybe they have been poring over a particular book for hours or asking to watch the same TV show repeatedly or they could just be asking a lot of questions around a certain topic. Most of all it is just being aware of what is interesting your child at the moment.

4

Lay The Foundation

Of course, there may be days when you have a great exhibit on but it is about a topic or artist that your child has no knowledge of. This doesn't mean they are going to hate it, it just means you need to do a bit of groundwork beforehand.

If I were to take you to a show of Takahashi Shunsuke*, you might be intrigued but you would hardly be excited (because you have no idea who he is). However, if I told you in advance that Takahashi Shunsuke is a top Japanese pop artist who worked alongside Andy Warhol and Keith Haring, has his work displayed in the MoMA New York and Tokyo and the National Art Museums in London and Paris and that he tragically died young in a freak art-related accident, then you are far more likely to want to go and see his work and find out more about him.

*Before you rush off to look up Takahashi Shunsuke, I totally made him up – it was just to prove a point!

You catch my drift though; with some teasers, some snippets of information, suddenly the show seems far more appealing. Even if you know very little about the exhibition you are planning to visit, the information on their website or listings in magazines will give you enough to 'leak' to your kids and get them intrigued about where they are going.

I know sometimes you end up rocking up to a museum on impulse, which makes laying groundwork so much more difficult, but if possible, gather some information about the artist/exhibit before you go and introduce them to your child…

Do you know which part of his body Van Gogh cut off?
Did you know some dinosaurs used to eat stones?
Did you know da Vinci designed a helicopter 400 years before one was ever built?
Can you guess what kind of animals Degas liked painting?

If you know well in advance then I recommend getting some books on the topic. I have included our favourites in the resources at the end of this book. YouTube is another good resource to utilize, as there are plenty of programs about every topic under the sun. I do recommend watching them first though to make sure they are suitable.

Often when a child has noticed something in a book or in a program, they get really excited about it when they see the real thing and will often make comments like,
"It's much bigger than I thought it would be" or "it looks much older than in the book".
Take note of their observations, they can lead you into a whole new conversation. The opposite also happens: if they have seen Van Gogh's Starry Night in real life and then see it in a book or in a film, they will often get excited about it.

5

Lay Down The Ground Rules

I think galleries and museums are very much like restaurants; if you go to a family-orientated fast food joint like MacDonalds, it is perfectly acceptable for your kids to be loud and run around the place. Other diners might not particularly like it but they will put up with it. But if you rock up to a 5 star Michelin restaurant and your kids behave in the same way, you are likely to alienate everyone else in there and quite possible get turfed out on your ear. Galleries and museums are the same: some are very child-orientated and it is fine to run around, get excited, touch things and squeal in delight but then there are places where similar behavior will get you shown to the exit before you can say Michelangelo.

If it's not a children's museum/exhibition you are visiting, then let your kids know beforehand. Talk about it on your way, then give them another reminder when you get there. Make your expectations clear before you even step foot inside. This is a good life lesson too, that certain behavior is expected in certain places and circumstances.

Some places are very hands-on and have plenty of things for the children to touch and feel, so you will need to explain why some items can't be touched and others can. Often they have made replicas for the interactive display, so simply explaining that the real deal can't be touched because it would soon get dirty or damaged should be enough.

Some children are happy to walk around like mini adults when it is required of them but some have more monkey-like instincts and would rather be swinging from the ceiling, if that is the case, go back to step 1 and find a place that is more suited to your child's temperament. This usually goes for the under 5's crowd, as the children get older they are more capable of behaviour that fits the situation.

I once saw a comment on a blog where the reader has her children take up 'the position', the one that serious gallery enthusiasts take on, hands clasped behind the back. I love the idea that the kids are mimicking accepted behavior and it has the added bonus of keeping sticky little fingers out of trouble.

Another thing which varies from place to place: some places allow children to take pencils in to fill in their trail sheets while other places (especially those who have priceless pieces of art on display) are strict on what you can and can't use. Popping a sketch pad and pencils in the bag just in case is a top idea and remember to ask permission before getting them out.

Food and drinks are also usually banned in gallery areas so it is worth having something to eat and drink before you go in, and explaining to the kids why they can't have anything once they get in there.

Sitting down should only be done on the seats provided and not on the edge of displays as this can set off alarm bells – yes, that is the voice of experience talking there!

Finally, grab yourself a map and learn the lay of the land, especially where the toilets and rest spots are in case your kiddies need a gallery break. Suggest checking out the toilets as soon as you arrive so you don't need a toilet break 10 minutes in! And a break at the gallery café can be a great incentive for good behavior when you are done.

6

Timing Is Everything

This is not so important for older kids but for little ones who still nap, you really need to take naps and feed times into consideration. When my son was still small enough to go in the carrier it wasn't that much of a big deal because he would fall asleep quickly if he was tired and being carried. When he got to three and a half – four though, he wasn't taking a nap every day but he would have some quiet time around 2.30 each afternoon. Trying to take him somewhere at that time of day could quickly turn nasty, so I tried to plan things for the morning and then at quiet time we would take a break. Paying attention to your child's routines and rhythms can help cut down on the meltdowns and tantrums.

If you have more than one child then it becomes a bit more of a juggling act, but not impossible. Observe your kids together during the normal day and see when they get on well together, when they need some time to run crazy, when they need quiet time and when they get grumpy. Again, a lot of this is common sense but we tend to forget about it when we leave the house!

Before you go in, see if there is a park or an area where the kids can let off steam a bit and get their wriggles out. Better to do that outside than in!

When you are actually there, pay attention to your child's mood. If you are getting signals that they have had enough, then leave. Visiting a gallery or museum should be a fun, enriching and rewarding experience, but it won't be any of those if you end with tantrums and meltdowns.

If the worst case scenario happens, yes, the dreaded tantrum, which is will at some stage, the best thing to do is to take it in your stride. Many places allow you to leave and enter again on the same day, so maybe taking a break and having a run around outside will calm the situation. If not, just leave and try again another day but when everyone has calmed down, try and figure out what the trigger was. It might be a simple case of over-tiredness or it could be that something in the exhibit scared them, take it as a lesson and try and work around it next time.

Tantrums are often cause by being tired, being hungry, being thirsty or not being able to communicate the problem. The first three issues you can almost always avoid by being organized, choosing the right time of day and making sure everyone has a full belly before you start. Not being able to communicate the problem is the one to cause problems and often the best way to deal with it is to change the scenery.

7

Making The Right Choice

Each child has his or her own personality and it really is worth taking that into consideration when choosing which museum or gallery to visit. If your child is one of those that are always on the go, can't do anything at any pace slower than a run, and loves to climb and jump, then taking them to a Degas exhibit in an upmarket gallery probably isn't the best choice. Instead, why not find a museum that is very hands-on; a lot of science and history museums are designed like that these days. Or if you are in need of your art fix, an outdoor sculpture park would be a great choice.

If you ever happen to be in Japan, the sculpture park in Hakone is amazing and actually has installations that the kids can climb on. They also have a couple of indoor galleries; if the kids have had a good run around they are usually worn out enough to be taken into the gallery without causing too much trouble!

Sculpture parks are a great way to introduce the child to the art world and they often don't have restrictions about food, drink and pencils. Many have picnic areas too so it makes a nice fun day out.

Many child-orientated galleries and museums hold classes and special lessons for children, another good thing to look into. Not only is this great for the kids but you are likely to meet other like-minded parents who can become friends for future trips. Your local gallery may have an annual pass which works well with kids, as you can make shorter, more frequent trips or even have a monthly museum day.

If you are planning on going to an exhibition with friends, then choose your friends wisely. This sounds a bit harsh but it can make a big difference to your enjoyment of the day. If you go to a gallery where children are expected to behave in a certain way (not run around like wild and crazy beasts) and you really want your child to appreciate the artwork, then choose like-minded parents who hold ideals similar to yours. If you end up gossiping all the way round while your kids run riot, you are going to be kicking yourself for paying out all that money when you could have gone to the park.

It could be that your child acts like an angel on their own but turns into a raving lunatic in the company of a certain friend. If you know this is likely to happen, better pick a different location for your playdate!

Of course, sometime the opposite happens. If both kids are obsessed with puzzles then they are likely to love the Escher exhibit and, with your encouragement, get a lot out of it. It might turn into a boast fest, with both kids trying to out-boast the other with their knowledge on the subject.

Choosing the right artist to see can make a difference too. Many children love the bright colours and bold painting of artists like Warhol, Haring and Kusama. Also, surrealists such as Salvador Dali grab the child's attention because of the weird and wonderful paintings, all melting clocks and long legged elephants. My son loves Picasso, as he puts it, "You can tell what the pictures are but they are a bit wonky and funny".

If you have a little ballerina then she might just fall in love with Degas or maybe your little wannabe engineer would find da Vinci the perfect subject matter? And don't forget your own passions. If you house is filled with Renaissance art then your kiddie is likely to enjoy an exhibit of Italian Renaissance artists; what fun to spot paintings that they already recognize and they will pick up on your enthusiasm too.

8

The Top Secret Trick

So far we have talked about the groundwork, deciding where and when to take your child. What has made a big difference in our family enjoyment of museums and galleries is the following…

Making it into a treasure hunt and throwing in some games

As I said in section 2, some museums and galleries have this covered which lets you off the hook but many of the galleries and museums we have been to just don't have this option. In Japan they often have a 'stamp rally' when the kids spend the whole time looking for the next stamp for their card rather than the exhibits, which makes me wonder what the whole point of going is!

I imagine that if you have got this far it's because you are a real art lover and you want your child to fall in love with art too, to appreciate the different styles, artists and techniques. So although this often means a bit of extra work on your behalf, it will make a world of difference to your trip.

I first did this when we were planning to go to a Picasso museum; at the time my son was about 4 and knew very little, if anything, about Picasso. We started off by buying a couple of books and reading them before we went and watching some short documentaries on YouTube. When we got to the museum I gave him the treasure hunt booklet and it was a big hit. He was focused and excited to find the answers to the questions, he was able to recognize pieces from The Blue Period and The Rose Period and he was very proud to be able to explain to daddy all about it. To this day, Picasso remains his favourite artist.

I have made a PDF for you to print out as a basic generic treasure hunt along with some other resources, you can download it here http://bit.ly/GandMSG

When you are visiting an exhibit which is focused on one artist, often they have information about the artist as part of the exhibit so the answers should be fairly easy to find. It goes without saying that the reading and writing ability of your child will play a part too. If you have more than one child you can either give them a sheet to do each or appoint one to do the writing. Take your kids' personalities into consideration, which is likely to work best for them?

General questions that are non-specific can be used for any artist:

- What is the artist's name?
- Where were they born?
- What style of art are they famous for?
- Which is your favourite painting? Why?
- When was the artist born?
- When did they die?
- What is an interesting fact you know about the artist?

With a little research before you go, you can ask specific questions about the work on show:

- When did he paint Starry Night?
- Which animals can you see in Guernica?

With even basic computer skills, you can add some images to your treasure hunt and get them looking for specific pieces as you make your way around.

Taking images from the Internet isn't really the proper way to go about this. I am explaining how I do it, but this technique really shouldn't be used for anything other than your own personal use. I am not a copyright lawyer but even I know that taking any images that you don't own and then selling them will land you in deep trouble.

First, Google the exhibit that you plan to go to. Often the gallery website will have a few pictures of things that will be on show and you can use those as a starting point. If there is an explanation of the artwork on display then use that and our friend Google to pick out a few more. 8 – 10 images are plenty: enough to make it into a treasure hunt without it getting boring or overwhelming.

I print our treasure hunts in landscape, fold them down the middle and staple them through the middle to make a little booklet. It is good to have a couple of blank pages for their own notes and sketches.

Encourage your child to write the date and name of the various works of art next to the images as they find them.

On occasion I have included pictures that turned out not to be on display, like when we went to the Andy Warhol exhibition and I included the iconic banana but it wasn't on show. Of course, it popped up in the museum shop so Ebi-kun checked it off his list any way.

By having the treasure hunt, the child is more engaged with the exhibit; they are scanning information looking for names and dates, taking note of paintings and what they are of. Their attention is drawn to what is in front of them.

There are going to be times when you don't have chance to lay the groundwork and prepare a book for them – don't panic!

Top Tip!

Visit the museum shop first, grab a few postcards of the work that is on display and use those as the visual clues for your treasure hunt. If that doesn't work for you, try the following games that can make the trip more interactive and fun. I bet your kids can come up with their own games too.

20 Questions

One person chooses one of the works of art in the room and the others have to guess which one by asking questions, but the questions can only have 'yes' or 'no' answers. The winner then gets to pick the artwork in the next room.

I Spy

An obvious contender, if the paintings are 'busy' then you can play just looking at one painting or, depending on the artwork on display, you might want to do it for the room.

Colour Hunt

Inspired by our nature walks, find all the different colours of the rainbow in order. The rule is one colour per artwork. My son loved doing this when he was a toddler. If it is a hands-off type of place you will have to remind them of the No Touching rule and even get them to take up 'the position'!

Going On A Picnic

A lot of artists have food in their artwork, so each time you see a new type of food add it to your imaginary picnic basket. When you get to the end, can you remember what is in there?

How Many...?

Keep a tally of all the … you see along the way, it could be little girls, dogs, apples…take your pick.

What the Dickens?

This is a fun game in museums with old artifacts or maybe futuristic inventions. Before anyone reads the information provided, you have to guess what the strange object is for.

- Is it a bed warmer?
- Is it for cooking bread in?
- Is it for carrying goods to market in?

Strike A Pose

If photography is allowed this can make for some fun pictures, but even without a camera it is fun. For artwork of people, get your kids to imitate the artwork. Can they stand in the same pose? Pull the same face? Expect giggling fits to ensue after this game, especially if mom and dad get in on the act too.

Another version of this is for one person to secretly choose an artwork and strike the pose while everyone else has to guess which piece of art they are imitating.

Family Vote

Everyone takes a minute or two to look at the same piece of art. When you are ready, everyone casts their vote. The choice is:

Heart – make a heart shape with your hands – this is for something that you love and would like to take home with you.

Thumbs up – Fonz style – this is for something
you like but not enough to want to take it home

Wavy-hands – hands flat, wave a little – this is for the pieces that are blah, so-so, you neither love it nor hate it.

Thumbs down – the inverted Fonz – this is for something you really don't like.

Once everyone has voted you can talk about your differences. I don't recommend you do this for every piece of art you come to, but maybe choose one from each room.

Can you find me…?

This game works well in a portrait gallery that isn't busy and with just one child or a group. Ask the kids to find… and then elicit stories out of them. It's a great way to develop their imagination too!

Can you find…?
* The prettiest lady
* The scariest man
* Someone who has a secret
* Somebody who likes sports
* Someone who is having a bad day

Snap, Snap

Not a game, but if the gallery allows photography, hand the camera over to the kids. It is interesting to see what captures their imagination, which pieces of art speak to them. Sometimes it is the whole thing and other times it can be a small detail that draws them in. Remember, kids are looking at the work from a different perspective; what they see in front of them is very different from how you see it.

Lastly, ask questions. Not in an 'in your face' teacher way but questions to make the child think more about what they are looking at. Open-ended questions with no right or wrong answer are a great way to develop the conversation...

- What do you think the people in the painting are talking about?
- If you could step into that painting, what would you do?
- Which direction is the sun coming from?*
- Do you know what you call this style of art?
- Does this artist's work remind you of anything else?
- How does this picture make you feel? Why?
- What type of paint was used by this artist?
- Which era is represented in this picture?
- (Use a point of reference in time that your child is familiar with, say the Second World War; is the picture representing time before or after the Second World War?)
- What are the people wearing? Do the clothes look comfortable?
- Who do you think she was? Was she important?
- Would you have liked to live in this era?
- Is there anything you recognize in the painting?
- Have you been to this place?

- Are all the people in this painting a family?
- How would the weather feel if you were in the painting?
- What do you think the person in the painting can smell?
- What do you think this was used for?
- What kind of mood was the artist in when he/she painted this?

*light plays an important role in paintings so it should be something that you bring up in conversation

9

The Museum Shop

Groan!
Actually, I love a quality museum shop!

We NEVER leave a museum shop without buying some postcards: portraits or self-portraits of the artist and/or works of art. Ebi-kun will pick out his favourite and I will usually pick out something famous. These don't get sent; they get added to our artists collection- more on that in a moment.

Sometimes, the museum shop can be a money trap so it is a good idea to set up some boundaries beforehand if you think it's likely to be an issue. Ebi-kun now has his own money and is more conscious of its value so I let him choose what he wants, if anything. Sometimes he will decide he doesn't want anything, other times he will fall in love with something, like the Andy Warhol Soup Can moneybox.

When he was younger I would put some guidelines in place; crap plastic toys were a no-go but if he wanted a book on something specific I would usually agree. This is obviously a totally personal thing, you might wish to skip the shop completely, just make sure your child knows the 'rules' before you get as far as the shop and you should be good! I have a friend who now has a great collection of fridge magnets from different exhibitions around the world. They pick one each visit and it serves as a reminder of the trip and as a conversation starter with her kids.

Back to the artists postcard collection... I have been doing this since Ebi-kun was a baby, so as you can imagine we have quite the collection now. Here are a few ideas of what you can do with the collection and of course, you can ask open-ended questions like the ones suggested earlier.

GAMES:

What's The Art?

Take it in turns to take a card, hide it from the other players and then describe it without mentioning the artist's name.
The other players have to guess the artist or name of the work.
The artist has a funny moustache
The picture is quite colourful.
It looks like a dream.
It has things melting in it.

Which Card?

Lay out the cards, face up on the floor or table.

Player one picks a card in their head but doesn't say which card it is. Then player one describes what is happening in the picture and the other players have to guess which card it is.

- There is water in the picture.
- It was painted in the olden days.
- **There are 3 ships in the painting...**

Which Card Version II (yes or no)

Lay out the cards, face up on the floor or table.
Player one picks a card in their head but doesn't say which card it is.
The other players take it in turns asking questions until someone guesses which card it is. The questions must be those with 'yes' or 'no' answers only.

- Is there a horse in the painting?
- Is there a woman in the painting?
- Is she crying?
- Is she wearing a blue dress?

What's The Link?

Spread out all the cards, then pick a few out and place them together in a group. The other players have to guess what the link is.

- It could be that all the pictures have a piece of fruit in them.
- They are all watercolour paintings.
- All the paintings have flowers in them.
- All the artists are French!

All the above games help the child remember the artist and the actual artwork. It also helps build vocabulary and expand their language skills. As you grow your collection they will start to recognize artists by their style.

Artist Picture Frames

What you need:

- 2 picture frames that allow the postcards to be slipped in from one side without having to take the back off (that makes it easier to change the cards).
- Some sticky-backed Velcro
- Marker pen
- Artist postcards
- Card

Cut a supply of card labels, approximately 2cm x 7cm (or whatever fits well on your frame, this is not an exact science!). It is worth making extra now so that when you buy more postcards you can simply add the details to the pre-made labels.
Cut your Velcro into strips a little smaller than your name labels. Stick the soft loops side to the backs of the name labels.

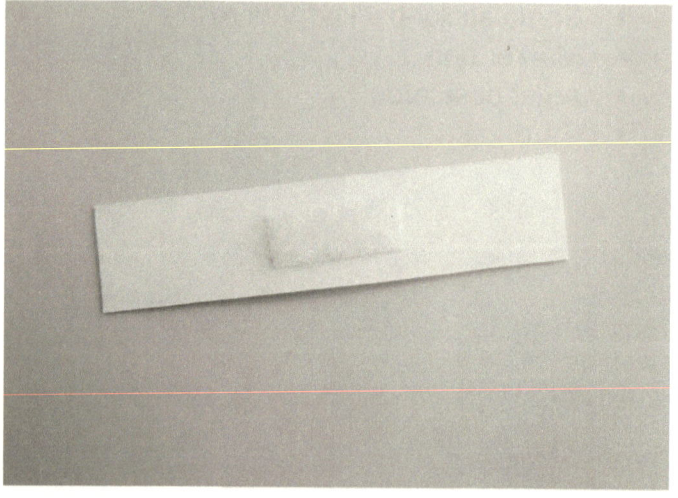

So that you can display all your cards, make one of the frames in landscape and the other in portrait. Cut a strip of Velcro and stick the rough side to the picture frame, at the bottom so that the name label can be attached to it.

Finally, write the name of the artist and the name of the artwork on each label and keep them in a bag or box along with the postcards.

Swap the cards around on a regular basis and challenge your child to find the right label for the artwork.

A visit to a museum or gallery shouldn't finish on the day. The gallery trip can be the starting point for a whole lot of exploration and fun!

There are also 2 sets of printable artists cards available in the free resource pack, you can download them here: http://bit.ly/GandMSG

Using the postcards and any pictures you have from the exhibition, take time to discuss the art with your child. Ask open ended questions such as...

- What kind of paint did the artist use?
- Why do you think he used this technique?
- How do you feel when you look at the painting?
- Why do you feel like that?
- What kind of mood was the artist in when he painted this?
- Do you think the artist liked the subject of the painting?
- Do you like the painting? Why or why not?
- Does the painting look realistic?*
- Do you think he is a good artist?

*Often children get frustrated because they don't know how to produce realistic looking pictures, but by looking at famous artists' work we can show them that realism isn't always important.

10

The Follow Up

It goes without saying that a trip to the gallery or museum should be followed up with some sort of art (or science) project. Try making your own art using the technique that the artist used.

The book Discovering Great Artists by Ann Marie Kohl has some great ideas and I have included some of my favourite resources in the back of this book and in the free resources gift page here: http://bit.ly/GandMSG

Once your child gets to the stage where they can write, encourage them to do a write-up of their trip, using the information they collected in the treasure hunt. They can also add bits from any brochures and the ticket as part of the write-up. This can be done in several ways, it could be in the style of a newspaper review or made into a booklet as a guide book for example.

Re-reading books about the artist becomes much more meaningful after a visit, and discussion can be continued as the child thinks more about the artwork she or he has seen. Remember to ask some open ended questions to get the discussion going.

Although the main purpose of this little book was to address taking a child to a museum or gallery, talking about art doesn't have to only happen there. We are surrounded by amazing art and design every day, from the packaging of juice cartons to the architecture of the train station. By pointing out these things and bringing them into everyday conversation it helps our children take a closer note of the beauty around us.

One hot topic at the moment is the use of photo-shopped models in advertising, which is most definitely a concern, but if children learn at a young age that these images are not real and can be compared to cartoon images or other computer generated artwork, then maybe we can save them the heartache of going down that road of comparing themselves to super skinny 'perfect' models. Try using the question...

How Do You Think They Did That?

This is one of my favourite bill board questions. I love the ideas that my son comes up with on how he thinks the art designs that the bill board uses are actually shot/made. Great for stretching little imaginations!

My final note – however you choose to approach your museum and gallery time, remember to keep it fun. We can make it educational without force-feeding them information or threatening to 'ask you questions when we get home'. It is our job as parents and educators to help our children fall in love with learning, to give them the tools that they need to quench their natural thirst for knowledge.

Resources

Books we love

Discovering Great Artists: Hands-On Art for Children in the Styles of the Great Masters By Mary Ann Kohl

Getting to Know the World's Greatest Artists Series by Mike Venizia (good for younger children)

The Katie books by James Meyhew

The Museums ABC book by The NY Metropolitan Museum Of Art
(there is also a shapes and numbers book in the same series)

13 Art Techniques Children Should Know by Angela Wenzel
(there are other 13... books available too)

The Artful Parent: Simple Ways to Fill Your Family's Life with Art and Creativity By Jean Van't Hul

Art Lab for Kids: 52 Creative Adventures in Drawing, Painting, Printmaking, Paper, and Mixed Media-For Budding Artists of All Ages by Susan Schwake

Red Ted Art : Cute and Easy Crafts for Kids by Maggy Woodley

Websites & Blogs We love

Google Cultural Institute
https://www.google.com/culturalinstitute/home?view=grid

The Artful Parent
http://artfulparent.com

Red Ted Art
http://www.redtedart.com

The Crafty Crow
http://www.thecraftycrow.net

Mrs Ricefield
http://www.mrsricefield.com/blog/

Contemporary Art daily
http://www.contemporaryartdaily.com

Art Project For Kids
http://www.artprojectsforkids.org

Deep Space Sparkle
http://www.deepspacesparkle.com

Big Kids Magazine
http://www.bigkidsmagazine.com

MoMA for kids
http://www.moma.org/interactives/destination/

British Museum Young Explorers
http://www.britishmuseum.org/explore/young_ex
plorers1.aspx

Virtual Sistine Chapel
http://www.vatican.va/various/cappelle/sistina_vr
/

Picassohead
http://www.picassohead.com/create.html

Don't Forget Your Free Gift

As a thank you for buying this book, I prepared some Montessori style art cards and a gallery treasure hunt printable along with a full list of resources. You just need to click over here to grab them - enjoy!

http://bit.ly/GandMSG

About The Author

Jo Ebisujima is a no-nonsense organizer and child-wrangler extraordinaire. She believes that a child's greatest teacher is his or her parent, and that the parent's job is to help the child fall in love with learning.

She's the best-selling author of Montessori Inspired Activities for Pre-Schoolers, where she draws on her Montessori experience to share 50+ activities that require no special equipment or training, and can be put together using items that you probably already own.

Jo is also the founder of My Organized Chaos where she helps busy mamas figure out what's not working and why. She understands how difficult it is to squeeze everything in, but she has an uncanny knack of showing you to break things down into do-able bite-sized chunks. With her no-BS attitude, she guides you on how to set up systems in your home so that everything runs more smoothly for you and your family.

Her love of travel and adventure have led her to live in far-flung places such as Israel, Ecuador and Italy. At one point she somehow she wound up in the northern wilderness of Japan, where she met her husband. She now lives just outside Tokyo with her husband and 8-year-old son, who is the inspiration for so much of her work.

When Jo is not writing or helping others, she can be found with her family out camping, visiting museums, or soaking up the atmosphere in an art gallery. She spends her free time at home sewing, designing, and generally making a crafty mess.

Where To Find Jo

Jo can be found all over the place, pop by and say hello...

My Organized Chaos Website:
http://www.my-organized-chaos.com

Personal Blog jojoebi designs:
http://www.jojoebi-designs.com

Facebook:
https://www.facebook.com/MyOrganizedChaosJo

Pinterest:
 http://www.pinterest.com/jojoebi/

Montessori Inspired Activities For Pre-Schoolers is available on Amazon and all good book stores.